We Like Fruit!

Written by Gill Budgell
Photographed by Steve Lumb

Collins

I like eating apples.

apples

I like eating bananas.

bananas

I like eating grapes.

grapes

I like eating oranges.

oranges

I like eating melons.

melons

11

We all like eating strawberries.

strawberries

13

Fruit

bananas

apples

grapes

oranges

melons

strawberries

☙ Ideas for guided reading ☙

Learning objectives: recognise printed words in a variety of settings, e.g. labels, captions; use a variety of cues when reading; make collections of words linked to particular topics; interact with others, negotiating plans and taking turns in conversation

High frequency words: I, like, we, all

Interest words: fruit, label, apples, bananas, grapes, oranges, melons, strawberries

Word count: 31

Curriculum links: Knowledge and Understanding of the World; Mathematical Development; Creative Development.

Resources: small whiteboard and pen, a bag of everyday fruit and vegetables

Getting started

- Put some fruit and vegetables on the table or floor and ask the children to identify them (*potato, carrot, onion, apple, orange, banana*)

- Ask the children to sort the foods into two piles: fruit and vegetables. Check whether they know the difference between fruit and vegetables.

- List all the fruit that children know on a whiteboard. Ask them when they like to eat fruit and which ones they like best.

- Look at the front cover. Ask the children to identify the fruit in the picture.

Reading and responding

- Read the words on the front and back cover together. Dwell on the word *fruit* and look carefully at the 'fr' blend at the beginning of the word and the 't' at the end of the word to help read it.

- Read pp2-3 together and rehearse reading *I like eating...* . Introduce the word *label* and read the word *apples* in the label. Ask the children to match the label on p3 with the word *apples* on p2.